The Lord's Praye.

Learning the Words Jesus Taught

by Adam Thomas

with text of the prayer from
The Book of Common Prayer (1979)
of The Episcopal Church

Photography courtesy of Unsplash.com

For permissions, please contact Adam Thomas through his website
wherethewind.com

Our Father,

Dear God,
Perfect Father and Mother
of all Creation,
including us,

who art in heaven,

You live above,
beyond, and within
all that you have made,

hallowed be
thy Name,

Your Name is set apart as special:

thy kingdom come,
thy will be done,
on earth as it is in heaven.

Help us make our world
a place of love, peace, and justice,
so it comes closer to the place
where your presence
is the fullness of joy.

Give us this day
our daily bread.

Give us what we need
to be our true selves today,
and help us not to use too much
of this world's precious resources.

And forgive us our trespasses,

Repair our relationships with you
when we are wrong or go astray,

as we forgive those
who trespass against us.

as we follow your example
in repairing relationships
when others wrong us.

And lead us not into temptation,

Keep us from doing things
that harm ourselves or others,

but deliver us from evil.

And give us strength
to stand against things
that seek to destroy
what you have made.

For thine is the kingdom,
and the power,
and the glory,
for ever and ever.

Amen.

You are more perfect and more loving
than we can possibly imagine,
and to you we devote our lives.
Thank you for listening to our prayer.

Our Father,
who art in heaven,
hallowed be thy Name,
thy kingdom come, thy will be done,
on earth as it is in heaven.
Give us this day our daily bread.
And forgive us our trespasses,
as we forgive those who trespass against us.
And lead us not into temptation,
but deliver us from evil.
For thine is the kingdom,
and the power, and the glory,
for ever and ever.
Amen.

Photographs

Lighthouse: Robert Wiedemann

Birds: Johannes Plenio

Trees: kazuend

Dandelion: Dawid Zawiła

Bread: James Harris

Sheep: Rod Long

Wall: Jonathan Bean

Desert: Tobias Keller

Waterfall: Joshua Sortino

Mountain: Jeremy Bishop

Stones: Aaron Thomas

All images from Unsplash.com